The Most Fa Aloha Recipes

The Best Flavors of The Hawaiian Cuisine
Gathered in One Cookbook

BY: Valeria Ray

License Notes

A Special Reward for Purchasing My Book!

Thank you, cherished reader, for purchasing my book and taking the time to read it. As a special reward for your decision, I would like to offer a gift of free and discounted books directly to your inbox. All you need to do is fill in the box below with your email address and name to start getting amazing offers in the comfort of your own home. You will never miss an offer because a reminder will be sent to you. Never miss a deal and get great deals without having to leave the house! Subscribe now and start saving!

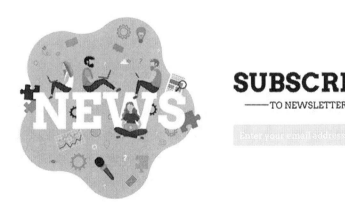

https://valeria-ray.gr8.com

Contents

Delicious Hawaiian Food Recipes

MMMMMMMMMMMMMMMMMMMMMMMMMMMMMMMMM

(1) Hawaiian Ham Fried Rice

Ham isn't only for big holiday dinners anymore. You can use it in meals for a few days afterward. It's great in quiche, casseroles and omelets. This fried rice recipe is so tasty that your family won't even be able to tell that it's made largely from leftovers.

Yield: 2-4 Servings

Preparation Time: 35 minutes

List of Ingredients:

- 1 cup of diced pineapple, fresh
- 4 cups of white rice, long-grain, cooked and cooled
- 2 lightly beaten eggs, large
- 1 tablespoon of ginger, fresh, minced
- 3 minced large cloves of garlic
- 1 diced yellow onion, medium
- 4 green onions, with sliced green parts and minced white parts
- 1 stemmed, de-seeded, cut bell pepper, red, large
- 1 & ½ cups of ham, chopped
- 1 tablespoon of oil, vegetable
- 1 tablespoon of Sriracha sauce
- 2 tablespoons of sesame oil, toasted
- 3 tablespoons of soy sauce

MMMMMMMMMMMMMMMMMMMMMMMMMMMMMMMM

Methods:

1. Whisk Sriracha, soy sauce and sesame oil together in small sized bowl. Set it aside.

2. Heat a tablespoons of vegetable oil in large skillet on med-high until barely smoking. Add the yellow onion, white parts from green onion, bell pepper and ham. Stir occasionally while cooking until the mixture is browned lightly. This should take six to eight minutes.

3. Add the ginger and garlic and stir while cooking until they are fragrant.

4. Add the eggs to the skillet. Combine into the mixture. Constantly stir until the eggs have cooked.

5. Add soy sauce mixture and rice to the skillet. Stir and combine until the rice has been heated completely through. Remove from heat. Add green parts of green onion and the pineapple and stir well. Serve promptly.

(2) Hawaiian Skillet Sausage

This recipe is a great choice for a day when you have some of the ingredients in your home already, but you're not sure how to best use them. You can adjust the sugar level to make it sweeter or less sweet.

Yield: 6 Servings

Preparation Time: 45 minutes

List of Ingredients:

- 1 x 16-oz. pkg. of cubed Polish sausage
- ¾ peeled, cored, cubed pineapple, fresh
- 1 sliced onion, large
- 1 tablespoon of oil, vegetable
- 1 cubed green bell pepper, large
- ½ cup of pineapple juice
- 2 tablespoons of corn starch
- 1/3 cup of brown sugar, packed
- 2 teaspoons of garlic, minced
- 2 tablespoons of soy sauce
- 1 & ¾ tablespoons vinegar, cider

MMMMMMMMMMMMMMMMMMMMMMMMMMMMMMMMM

Methods:

1. Heat the oil in large-sized skillet on med. heat. Stir and cook bell pepper, sausage and onion until veggies begin to become tender.

2. Add the pineapple. Stir occasionally while cooking until pineapple is hot.

3. Whisk the corn starch and pineapple juice together. Stir the garlic, soy sauce, vinegar and brown sugar with pineapple juice until sugar has dissolved. Pour on top of sausage mixture. Cook until sauce has thickened. Serve.

(3) Hawaiian Slow-Cooked Meatballs

These are similar to meatballs made with BBQ sauce and jelly, but the pineapple juice gives them a Hawaiian flavor. They can be served on rice with scallions over the top if you use them for a main dish. You can also serve them as an appetizer.

Yield: 25 BBQ meatballs

Preparation Time: 10 minutes

List of Ingredients:

- 1 cup of barbeque sauce
- 1 x 8-oz. can of pineapple, sliced
- 25 meatballs, frozen

MMMMMMMMMMMMMMMMMMMMMMMMMMMMMMMMMM

Methods:

1. Add meatballs to slow cooker. Pour barbeque sauce on top. Add pineapple and juice. Cook on med-high for two to three hours.

2. Enjoy alone or serve on rice for main dish.

(4) Aloha Overnight Oats

This is such a simple breakfast recipe. Just start with an equal amount of oats and milk, add sweet, shredded coconut and a bit of brown sugar. Time does the mixing of flavors for you, since it sits overnight.

Yield: 2 Servings

Preparation Time: 10 minutes

List of Ingredients:

- ¼ cup of macadamia nuts, chopped
- ½ cup of diced pineapple, fresh
- ¼ cup of cherries, dried
- ½ tablespoons of sugar, brown
- 1 cup of oats, old-fashioned
- ¼ cup of shredded coconut, sweetened
- 1 cup of milk, low-fat

MMMMMMMMMMMMMMMMMMMMMMMMMMMMMMMMM

Methods:

1. Stir cherries, sugar, coconut, milk and oats together in a large sized bowl. Divide mixture in two-pint, lidded jars.

2. Cover. Refrigerate for six to eight hours, or simply refrigerate overnight.

3. Stir oats. Top jars with macadamia nuts and pineapple. Serve.

(5) Lilikoi Pie

This is quite simply the ultimate in tropical pies. The local passion fruit, lilikoi, is not always easily found, but if you have fruit markets locally, it's worth your time. Or you can use canned passion fruit. You can also serve this with whipped cream.

Yield: 8 Servings

Preparation Time: 3 hours & 55 minutes including 2 hours of refrigeration time

List of Ingredients:

- 1 x 9" graham cracker crust, prepared
- 1 & 1/3 cup of sugar, white
- 4 egg yolks
- 4 egg whites
- 2 teaspoons of lemon zest, grated
- ¼ cup of water, cold
- 1 tablespoon of gelatin, unflavored
- ½ cup of juice, passion fruit
- ½ teaspoons of salt, kosher

MMMMMMMMMMMMMMMMMMMMMMMMMMMMMMMM

Methods:

1. In top pan of double boiler, combine fruit juice, salt, 1/3 cup of sugar and the egg yolks. Cook on low and stir until it thickens.

2. Dissolve the gelatin in water and stir it into the yolk mixture until the gelatin dissolves.

3. Add lemon zest and stir. Turn heat off. Allow to cool until it congeals slightly.

4. In large sized mixing bowl, beat the egg whites until they become foamy. Add 1 cup of white sugar gradually and beat until you see the formation of stiff peaks.

5. Fold the egg whites gently into yolk mixture until you can no longer see any streaks. Spoon this into the pie crust. Place in your fridge for two hours to firm up. Serve.

(6) Hawaiian Bacon, Egg & Cheese Sliders

This is an easy recipe that can feed lots of people, without you having to spend a ton of time in front of the oven. You can make parts of these little sandwiches ahead of time. They travel well and you don't need utensils to eat them.

Yield: 8 Servings

Preparation Time: 35 minutes

List of Ingredients:

- 1 tablespoon of butter, melted
- ½ lb. of cooked bacon
- 4 scrambled eggs, large
- ¼ cup of cheddar cheese, shredded
- 1/8 cup or less of mayonnaise
- 8 bread rolls, Hawaiian

MMMMMMMMMMMMMMMMMMMMMMMMMMMMMMMMMMM

Methods:

1. Preheat the oven to 350F.

2. Cut rolls in middle to create buns.

3. Spread mayo on bottoms of buns. Place bread in 8-inch x 8-inch square metal pan.

4. Layer eggs, cheese and cooked bacon on bottoms of buns.

5. Put tops on buns. Brush with melted butter.

6. Cover pan. Bake for 10 minutes. Remove foil. Cook for two more minutes.

7. Cut into 12-16 small-sized sandwiches. Serve.

(7) Coconut Pineapple Lush

This Hawaiian-inspired coconut and pineapple lush celebrates all kinds of flavor combinations. There is only a short baking time and you'll create a decadent dessert laced with melted butter, chocolate chips, macadamia nuts and coconut.

Yield: 16 Servings

Preparation Time: 5 hours and 10 minutes including 4 hours chilling time

List of Ingredients:

- 16 cherries, maraschino
- 4 cups of milk, whole
- 2 x 3.4-ounce packages of pudding mix, coconut, instant
- 1 x 16-ounce container of thawed whipped topping
- 1 x 8-ounce can of drained pineapple, crushed
- 1 cup of sugar, confectioner's
- 2 x 8-ounce packages of softened cream cheese
- ½ cup of melted butter
- ½ cup coconut, flaked, sweetened
- 1/3 cup of chocolate chips, white
- ½ cup of chopped macadamia nuts
- 1 & ¾ cups of vanilla wafers, crushed

MMMMMMMMMMMMMMMMMMMMMMMMMMMMMMMMM

Methods:

1. Preheat the oven to 350F. Spray bottom of 13x9" baking dish using non-stick spray.

2. Toss melted butter, ¼ of coconut flakes, chocolate chips, macadamia nuts and vanilla wafer crumbs together in medium bowl.

3. Press on bottom of 13x9" baking dish and bake for 20 to 25 minutes until it sets. Allow to fully cool.

4. Increase oven temp. to broil. Spread last of coconut on medium baking sheet. Toast and stir for four to five minutes. Watch as it toasts, so it doesn't burn. Then allow to cool.

5. Whip powdered sugar and cream cheese together in medium bowl with a mixer. Add 1/3 of whipped topping and crushed pineapple and mix by hand. Spread over crust.

6. In same medium bowl, whip milk and pudding mix until it slightly thickens but can still be poured. Pour this over layer of pineapple.

7. Frost top with the rest of the whipped topping. Use maraschino cherries and toasted coconut to garnish. Chill and allow to set for four hours. Serve.

(8) Hawaiian Monkey Bread

This is the easiest monkey bread you will probably ever make. You don't have to wait for the bread to rise, and the baking time is quite short, since the recipe makes use of sweet Hawaiian dinner rolls.

Yield: 4 Servings

Preparation Time: 20 minutes

List of Ingredients:

- ¾ cup of packed sugar, brown
- 1 stick of melted butter
- ½ cup of walnuts, chopped
- 1 teaspoon of cinnamon
- ½ cup of sugar, granulated
- 1 beaten egg, large
- 1 pkg. of rolls, sweet dinner type

MMMMMMMMMMMMMMMMMMMMMMMMMMMMMMMM

Methods:

1. Preheat the oven to 350F. Spray Bundt pan using non-stick spray.

2. Mix sugar and cinnamon in small-sized bowls. Cut dinner rolls into four to six pieces each. Place them in large sized bowl.

3. Pour egg on bread. Use your hands to toss it. Pour the sugar/cinnamon on bread and egg mixture. Again, use your hands to toss. Place the mixture in Bundt pan.

4. Sprinkle walnuts on top of bread mixture.

5. Stir brown sugar and melted butter together. Pour over pan mixture evenly. Bake for 12-15 minutes. Allow to cool in the pan.

6. Run knife around pan edges and pan center. This will release bread. Place plate on top of pan. Tip to serve.

(9) Aloha Butter Mochi

Butter mochi is so incredibly easy to make. The measurements are not exact, since you're mainly using cans. After you mix, then pour and bake, then you cut, and voila! It is not a healthy dessert, but everyone needs to indulge once in a while.

Yield: 10 Servings

Preparation Time: 1 hour & 20 minutes

List of Ingredients:

- 1 x 14-ounce can of milk, coconut
- 1 x 12-ounce can of milk, evaporated
- 2 teaspoons of baking powder
- 1 lb. of flour, mochiko (sweet rice)
- 1 teaspoon of vanilla extract
- 4 eggs, large
- 2 cups of sugar, granulated
- 1 stick of melted butter, unsalted

MMMMMMMMMMMMMMMMMMMMMMMMMMMMMMMMMMM

Methods:

1. Preheat the oven to 350F. Grease 13x9" pan.

2. Mix sugar and melted butter and combine. Add eggs and mix after each egg.

3. Add vanilla and stir. Pour in mochiko flour and baking powder. Stir until almost fully combined.

4. Add evaporated milk and coconut milk and stir in. When the batter is completely smooth, then pour it into the pan. Bake for 60 minutes.

5. Remove from the oven. Sit to cool. Remove it from pan. Cut and serve.

(10) Hawaiian Omelet

This is a super easy and quick breakfast recipe that gives you the taste of the islands without a lot of work. You can use mozzarella cheese if you prefer. Either mozzarella or cheddar cheese combine well with the ham and pineapple.

Yield: 2-3 Servings

Preparation Time: 15 minutes

List of Ingredients:

- ½ cup of shredded Monterey jack cheese
- 6 tablespoons of water, filtered
- ½ cup of shredded cheese, cheddar
- 6 medium eggs
- ½ cup of ham, cubed
- 1/3 cup of chunked pineapple
- Sea salt & ground pepper, as desired

MMMMMMMMMMMMMMMMMMMMMMMMMMMMMMMMMM

Methods:

1. Beat water, eggs, sea salt & ground pepper together.

2. Coat skillet thinly with cooking spray. Heat on med-high.

3. Pour the egg mixture in pan. When eggs have almost fully set, sprinkle ½ pf omelet with the other ingredients.

4. Fold second half of the omelet over the filling. Continue to cook until the cheese is melted. Cut the omelet into three wedges. Serve.

(11) Pineapple Upside Down Cake

This recipe comes from a native Hawaiian. It is best made with fresh pineapple, and it is especially tasty when served with whipped cream or ice cream.

Yield: 8 Servings

Preparation Time: 1 hour & 45 minutes

List of Ingredients:

- ¾ cup of milk, whole
- 1 teaspoon of vanilla extract, pure
- 2 eggs, large
- 2/3 cup of sugar, white
- ½ cup of softened butter, unsalted
- ½ teaspoons of cinnamon, ground
- 1 & ½ cups of flour, all-purpose
- 3 cups of cored, peeled and chunked pineapple, fresh
- 2/3 cup of brown sugar, packed
- ½ teaspoons of salt, kosher
- 1 & ½ teaspoons of baking powder

MMMMMMMMMMMMMMMMMMMMMMMMMMMMMMMMM

Methods:

1. Preheat oven to 350F.

2. Stir brown sugar and melted butter together in small sized bowl. Evenly spread mixture in buttered, round 9" cake pan.

3. Pat pineapple dry with paper towels. Arrange on sugar mixture.

4. Sift cinnamon, salt, baking powder and flour together.

5. Cream softened butter with sugar in large sized bowl until mixture is fluffy and light. Add eggs and beat after you add each one.

6. Stir in vanilla. Add flour mixture and milk in three alternating batches. Beat after every addition. Evenly spread batter into pan.

7. Place cake pan in middle of oven. Bake for 40-55 minutes. Allow to cool for about 15 minutes on a rack. Invert onto plate. Serve warm.

(12) Hawaiian Pancakes

These pancakes from the Hawaiian Islands are so fluffy! They are loaded with macadamia nuts, pineapple and coconut, so they give you authentic taste from the aloha state.

Yield: 8 Servings

Preparation Time: 1 hour + overnight refrigeration

List of Ingredients:

- 1 & ½ cup of coconut, shredded
- 3 teaspoons of baking powder
- 1 & ½ cup of chopped macadamia nuts
- 3 eggs, whites separated from the yokes
- 1 teaspoon of pure vanilla extract
- ¾ cup of pineapple, crushed, from can
- 1 & ¼ cup of milk, whole
- ¾ cup of sugar, granulated
- 2 & ¼ cups of flour, all-purpose
- 1 pinch of salt

To Top: maple syrup

MMMMMMMMMMMMMMMMMMMMMMMMMMMMMMM

Methods:

1. Make batter the evening before you want to enjoy this breakfast.

2. Whisk salt, sugar, flour and baking powder in large-sized bowl.

3. Whisk egg yolks, vanilla, pineapple and milk in a separate bowl until the mixture is smooth.

4. Pour wet mixture into dry mixture. Whisk together to create a thickened batter.

5. In a 3rd separate bowl, whip egg whites until they are fluffy, then form peaks.

6. Fold egg whites, 1 cup coconut and 1 cup macadamia nuts into remainder of the batter. Cover bowl. Refrigerate overnight.

7. The following morning, pre-heat oven to 350F. Prepare a large sized griddle.

8. Line baking sheet with silicone mat. Spread other half of coconut on it. Then toast in oven for three to five minutes until it is golden and crisp. Set pan aside.

9. Pre-heat griddle pan on med-high. Grease using butter. Cook pancake batter in the size of batches you prefer. Four minutes on each side will make them golden and puffy.

10. Sprinkle on coconut, macadamia nuts and top with maple syrup. Serve.

Now let's look at some tasty lunch, dinner and appetizer recipes... all made with Hawaiian flair...

(13) Hawaii Chocolate Haupia Pie

Haupia is among the favorites in aloha desserts. It's gelatinous and sweet, and made mainly from coconut milk. The recipe for this pie combines that popular dessert with decadent chocolate and a pie crust for an irresistible treat.

Yield: 6-8 Servings

Preparation Time: 1 hour & 55 minutes including 1 hour of refrigeration time

List of Ingredients:

- ¾ cup of chocolate, Dutch
- ½ cup of corn starch
- ¼ cup of granulated sugar
- 1 & ½ cups of cream, heavy
- 1 cup of water, filtered
- 1 cup of sugar, granulated
- 1 tablespoon of coconut extract, pure
- 1 x 14-ounce can of milk, coconut
- 1 cup of milk, whole
- 1 x 9-inch pie crust, unbaked

MMMMMMMMMMMMMMMMMMMMMMMMMMMMMMMM

Methods:

1. Preheat the oven to 350F. Bake the pie crust for 12-15 minutes. Set it aside and allow for cooling.

2. Whisk sugar, coconut extract, coconut milk and milk together in medium-sized pan.

3. Dissolve corn starch in filtered water in medium-sized bowl.

4. Bring coconut milk mixture to boil. Reduce and allow to simmer while you whisk in corn starch mixture. Keep stirring on low heat until the mixture thickens.

5. Divide into two individual sized bowls. In a separate bowl, microwave the chocolate until it melts.

6. Mix the chocolate in one of the coconut pudding bowls. Pour into pie crust. Spread out and allow to sit.

7. Pour other bowl of coconut pudding atop mixture in crust. Spread and smooth, but don't mix the layers. Refrigerate pie for at least an hour.

8. Whip heavy cream with sugar until it is stiff. Layer pie with whipped cream. Use chocolate shavings to garnish. Serve.

(14) Shoyu Chicken

The ingredients for this chicken recipe are very often found in your pantry or freezer, so you might be able to make it without a trip to your local grocery. It has the best taste if it's marinated overnight.

Yield: 4 Servings

Preparation Time: 35 minutes

List of Ingredients:

- 4 x 6-oz. cubed boneless, skinless chicken breasts
- 1 teaspoon of molasses
- 1 tablespoon of rice vinegar, Japanese
- 1 tablespoon of mirin
- 1 x 2" piece peeled & minced ginger, fresh
- 3 minced cloves of garlic
- ½ cup of beer, light
- ¼ cup of soy sauce
- ½ cup of brown sugar, packed
- 1 cup of rice, jasmine

To garnish: sliced green onions

MMMMMMMMMMMMMMMMMMMMMMMMMMMMMMMMMM

Methods:

1. Cook rice by directions on package in small sized pot.

2. Combine 1 cup water with molasses, vinegar, mirin, ginger, garlic, beer, soy sauce and sugar in medium sized pot. Bring to boil on med-high. Boil for 8-10 minutes. Sauce will thicken.

3. Reduce heat to low. Add chicken. Leave uncovered and simmer for about 10 minutes. Chicken must be cooked all the way through.

4. Season using salt. Garnish with the green onions and serve on rice.

(15) Grilled Swordfish & Salsa

Swordfish steaks work so well in grilling, since they don't fall apart, and they keep their pleasing texture. This dish has a mild, slightly sweet taste. It is especially tempting when paired with fruit salsa.

Yield: 2 Servings

Preparation Time: 35 minutes

List of Ingredients:

- 1 tablespoon of honey, pure
- 2 tablespoons of oil, olive
- 5 chopped leaves, basil
- ½ chopped red pepper
- 1 diced tomato
- 1 chopped avocado
- 1 sliced peach
- 2 x 8-oz. steaks, swordfish
- 1 squeezed lime
- 5 chopped mint leaves
- Greens, fresh
- Salt, kosher
- Pepper, ground

MMMMMMMMMMMMMMMMMMMMMMMMMMMMMMMMMMM

Methods:

1. Prepare fruit salsa. Mix mint, basil, red pepper, tomato, avocado, peach, honey, lime juice and 1 tablespoon olive oil. Season using salt and ground pepper. Combine well. Set the bowl aside.

2. Preheat grill to med. Drizzle swordfish with ½ tablespoons olive oil each. Season using salt & pepper.

3. Grill swordfish for five to six minutes on each side.

4. Arrange the greens on plates. Top with swordfish. Spoon fruit salsa on fish. Serve.

The Hawaiian Islands offer a wide variety of scrumptious desserts. Here are some wonderful recipes...

(16) Hawaiian Ahi Poke

This poke recipe is so easy that you can make it fairly easily and it will still taste a lot like the poke they serve in restaurants in the aloha state. The most important aspect is the use of fresh tuna – the freshest you can find. In your area, that may mean using frozen tuna, which is fine.

Yield: 4 Servings

Preparation Time: 2 hours & 20 minutes including 2 hours refrigeration time

List of Ingredients:

- 1 lb. of cubed yellowfin ahi tuna, sushi-grade
- 1 tablespoon of dried seaweed, crumbled
- 2 tablespoons of macadamia nuts, roasted, crushed
- ½ teaspoons of pepper flakes, red, hot
- 1 teaspoon of sesame seeds, toasted
- ½ teaspoons of salt, as desired
- 1/3 cup of green onions, sliced thinly, + extra to serve
- 1 teaspoon of ginger root, fresh, grated
- 2 tablespoons of oil, sesame
- ¼ cup of soy sauce

To serve: rice vinegar, lemon juice or lime juice

MMMMMMMMMMMMMMMMMMMMMMMMMMMMMMMMM

Methods:

1. Whisk together the salt, pepper flakes, seaweed, nuts, onions, ginger, sesame oil and soy sauce in medium bowl.

2. Place tuna cubes in a separate bowl. Pour marinade in. Stir and evenly coat tuna. Cover. Refrigerate for two hours and mix once more.

3. Top with green onions, sesame seeds, and sprinkle the top with rice vinegar, lime or lemon juice. Serve.

(17) Hawaiian Hay Stacks

These haystacks have been a favorite with youngsters and adults alike, growing up in the islands. You can basically use the main ingredients and build the dish as you prefer.

Yield: 2-3 Servings

Preparation Time: 15 minutes

List of Ingredients:

- 1 can of soup, cream of chicken
- 2-3 chunked, cooked chicken breasts
- ½ cup of sour cream
- 1 cup of broth, chicken
- 3 to 4 cups of rice, steamed
- Pepper, ground, as desired

To garnish: choose your favorites

- Diced tomatoes
- Chow Mein noodles
- Chopped green pepper
- Chopped celery
- Chopped green ònions
- Olives, sliced
- Almonds, slivered
- Cheese, grated
- Mandarin oranges
- Pineapple tidbits
- Flaked coconut

MMMMMMMMMMMMMMMMMMMMMMMMMMMMMMMMMM

Methods:

1. Combine the chicken broth and soup, creating gravy. Add chunks of chicken. Simmer for about 10 minutes. Then stir in sour cream.

For serving:

Place rice on individual plates. Top with gravy, cheese, then chow Mein noodles, plus others on the list of garnishes, as you prefer. Top it off using teriyaki or soy sauce.

(18) Aloha Pork Bowl

The delectable tastes in this dish are brought out by marinating the pork in semi-sweet tea before you grill it. The marinated pork is the star in this rice bowl, which also includes onions, pineapples and lime dressing.

Yield: 4 Servings

Preparation Time: 45 minutes + 1-hour refrigeration time

List of Ingredients:

- 1 x 1-lb. butterflied, flattened pork tenderloin
- 2 tea bags, English breakfast
- 3 x ½" thick peeled, cored, quartered fresh pineapple slices
- 2 tablespoons of cilantro, minced, + extra sprigs to serve
- ¼ cup of lime juice, fresh
- 1/3 cup of olive oil, + extra to brush on
- 2 "cut in wedges" red onion
- ¼ cup of sugar, granulated
- 1 cup of water, boiling
- Sea salt & ground pepper

To serve: sliced jalapeño, diced avocado, crisp bacon, steamed rice

MMMMMMMMMMMMMMMMMMMMMMMMMMMMMMMM

Methods:

1. Combine tea bags, boiling water and sugar in large sized bowl. Allow to sit for about five minutes.

2. Discard tea bags. Stir tea and dissolve sugar. Allow to completely cool. Add pork. Place in refrigerator for about an hour.

3. Preheat large grill pan. Drain pork. Pat dry using paper towels. Brush onion, pork and pineapple with oil. Season using salt and ground pepper.

4. Grill pork on high and turn once. It should char lightly.

5. Transfer pork to cutting board. Allow to sit for about five minutes. Slice pork.

6. Grill onion and pineapple and turn once until they are charred.

7. Whisk 1/3 cup of oil, lime juice and cilantro in a small sized bowl. Season with sea salt & ground pepper.

8. Serve pineapple, onion and pork on steamed rice. Top with lime dressing, jalapeño, diced avocado and crisp bacon, if desired.

(19) Pineapple Vinaigrette Salad

This is such an easy salad, using bagged greens, coconut, nuts, bacon bits and pineapple. It tastes best when served with fresh pineapple, but canned works, too. You can use almonds instead of macadamia nuts, if you prefer.

Yield: 2-3 Servings

Preparation Time: 1/2 hour

List of Ingredients:

- ¼ cup of toasted coconut flakes
- 3 chopped green onions
- ½ cup of toasted, chopped macadamia nuts
- 1 cup of fresh pineapple, diced
- 1 x 10-oz. pkg. of romaine lettuce, chopped
- ¼ cup of oil, olive
- 3 tablespoons of vinegar, red wine
- ¼ cup of pineapple juice
- 6 slices of lean bacon
- Sea salt, as desired
- Ground pepper, as desired

MMMMMMMMMMMMMMMMMMMMMMMMMMMMMMMMMM

Methods:

1. Place the bacon in large sized skillet. Cook on med-high until browned evenly. Drain the bacon, crumble it, and set it aside.

2. Combine the salt, oil, pepper, vinegar and pineapple juice in a cruet or a jar with lid. Cover. Shake well to combine.

3. Toss the lettuce, bacon, green onions, macadamia nuts and pineapple together in large sized bowl. Add dressing and toss. Use coconut for garnish and serve.

(20) Hawaiian Cheese Bread

You may fall in love with this Hawaiian version of cheese bread – it's SO delicious! Take it to a work party or picnic and watch it disappear. It's quick and easy to make, and almost everyone who has tasted it loves it.

Yield: 8 Servings

Preparation Time: 45 minutes

List of Ingredients:

- ¼ cup of melted butter
- 2 slices of chopped onion, red
- 4 oz. of cheese, Swiss
- ½ loaf of sweet bread, Hawaiian
- ½ teaspoons of sea salt, coarse
- 1 & ½ cloves of minced garlic

MMMMMMMMMMMMMMMMMMMMMMMMMMMMMMMMM

Methods:

1. Cut the bread into one-inch slices diagonally. Repeat the cuts in the opposite direction.

2. Cut cheese into ¼" slices and cut those slices into smaller pieces. Insert in the bread.

3. Combine salt, garlic, butter and onion and spoon the mixture over the bread.

4. Wrap the loaf in aluminum foil. Bake for 20-30 minutes at 350F. Cheese should be melted before serving, warm.

(21) Aloha Burgers

This recipe is well worth the little time it takes to fire up your grill. You'll be creating Hawaiian mini burgers. These sliders are temptingly flavored using BBQ sauce, and they are usually served on Hawaiian sweet rolls, along with bacon, cheese and pineapple.

Yield: 12 Sliders

Preparation Time: 40 minutes

List of Ingredients:

- 6 bacon slices
- 1 x 8-ounce can of sliced, drained pineapple with juice reserved
- 3 quartered slices of cheese, Swiss
- 1 package of dinner rolls, Hawaiian
- ¾ teaspoons of steak seasoning, Montreal
- 3 tablespoons of breadcrumbs
- 2/3 cup of BBQ sauce, brown sugar
- 1 & 1/2 -lb. of ground chuck
- Lettuce

MMMMMMMMMMMMMMMMMMMMMMMMMMMMMMMMM

Methods:

1. Spray gas grill grate with cooking spray. Preheat to medium.

2. Combine 2 tablespoons of pineapple juice with BBQ sauce.

3. Combine 1/3 cup of the BBQ mixture with bread crumbs, steak seasoning and bread crumbs in a large sized bowl. Shape into 12 patties.

4. Place the pineapple slices in a bowl with the rest of the BBQ sauce. Set aside.

5. Grill the patties for three or four minutes each side until they have cooked all the way through.

6. Remove rolls from the package but don't separate. Slice in halves, horizontally. Spray the cut sides using cooking spray and toast them on the grill.

7. Remove the sliced pineapple from the sauce. Grill for a couple minutes per side.

8. Separate the rolls. Assemble the burgers. Spread the rest of the BBQ sauce on the rolls. Lay a lettuce leaf and patties on bottoms. Top using cheese, pineapple and bacon. Close tops of the rolls and serve.

(22) Huli Huli Chicken with Pineapple

In Hawaii, you will find this type of BBQ chicken at local roadside stands. You will use brown sugar and crushed pineapple, which offer you wonderful flavor in a caramelized texture.

Yield: 12 Servings

Preparation Time: 5 hours & 40 minutes including 4 hours of marinating time

List of Ingredients:

- 3 x 3.5-lb. quartered frying chickens
- 1 minced garlic clove
- 1x1-inch piece of minced ginger, fresh
- ¼ cup of Worcestershire sauce
- 1/3 cup of red wine
- ¾ cup of sugar, brown
- 1 x 20-oz. can of pineapple, crushed, with juice
- 1/3 cup of ketchup
- ½ cup of soy sauce, Japanese (shoyu)

MMMMMMMMMMMMMMMMMMMMMMMMMMMMMMMM

Methods:

1. Stir the Worcestershire sauce, garlic, ginger, red wine, ketchup, shoyu, brown sugar and pineapple together in large pot. Bring to boil and lower heat to med-low.

2. Stir occasionally while simmering until sauce has been reduced and it thickens. This should take about a half-hour. Allow to cool. Transfer 1 & ½ cups of this sauce into a medium bowl. Refrigerate.

3. Place the chicken pieces in large sized bowl. Pour the rest of the sauce on top and toss to coat evenly. Cover bowl with cling wrap. Marinate in your fridge for at least four hours, or overnight.

4. Preheat grill to med-high. Oil grate lightly.

5. Remove the chicken from the marinade and discard the rest of the marinade. Cook chicken on grill until it caramelizes. This takes approximately five minutes for each side.

6. Reduce the grill heat to low. Turn and baste while cooking with 1 & ½ cups of the pineapple sauce, 'til the juice runs clear and chicken has no pink color. Serve promptly.

(23) Papaya & Tomato Salad

Everyone seems to love the crunch of Hawaii's green papayas. This salad uses them well, along with grape tomatoes, healthy greens and lots of herbs.

Yield: 10-12 Servings

Preparation Time: 45 minutes

List of Ingredients:

- 1-lb. of cut green beans, 2" long
- 10 cups of green papaya, julienned, packed lightly
- 2 cups of tomatoes, grape
- 5 Thai chilies, small
- ½ cup of macadamia nuts
- ¼ cup of fish sauce, Asian
- 2 cloves of garlic
- ½ cup of lime juice, fresh
- 1 teaspoon of lime zest, grated finely
- ½ cup of cilantro leaves, packed lightly
- 1 teaspoon of salt, kosher
- ½ cup sliced basil
- 2 tablespoons of honey, pure

MMMMMMMMMMMMMMMMMMMMMMMMMMMMMMMMM

Methods:

1. Preheat oven to 350F.

2. Toast nuts 'til golden in pie plate. Allow to cool and chop coarsely.

3. Combine fish sauce, salt, honey, lime juice, lime zest, garlic and chilies in food processor. Puree until the mixture is smooth.

4. Toss papaya, cilantro, basil, tomatoes and green beans in medium sized bowl. Add vinaigrette. Toss once more. Fold in nuts. Serve.

(24) Aloha Chicken Pineapple Kebabs

Hawaiian kebabs are in their own class when it comes to tropical taste sensations. These are delicious, tender and sweet. You won't need many ingredients, so they're quite easy to make.

Yield: 8 Servings

Preparation Time: 2 hours & 40 minutes

List of Ingredients:

- 1 x 20-oz. can of drained pineapple chunks
- 8 boneless, skinless halved chicken breasts, cut into small pieces
- 1 tablespoon of oil, sesame
- 2 tablespoons of sherry
- 3 tablespoons of sugar, brown
- ¼ teaspoons of garlic powder
- 2 & ¾ tablespoons of soy sauce
- ¼ teaspoons of ginger, ground

MMMMMMMMMMMMMMMMMMMMMMMMMMMMMMMMMM

Methods:

1. Mix garlic powder, ginger, sesame oil, sherry, brown sugar and soy sauce in shallow dish.

2. Stir pineapple and chicken pieces into marinade and coat well. Cover. Marinate in fridge for two hours or more.

3. Preheat your grill to med-high. Oil grill grate lightly.

4. Thread pineapple and chicken on skewers. Grill for 15-20 minutes and turn occasionally. Serve warm.

(25) Honey-Pineapple Hawaiian Shrimp

If you love pineapple, this is a great dish to use it in. The taste combinations are wonderful. The recipe itself is simple and easy, making use mainly of pineapples, honey and soy sauce.

Yield: 4 Servings

Preparation Time: 15 minutes

List of Ingredients:

- 1 tablespoon of mint, chopped freshly
- 1 cup of chunked pineapple
- 1 tablespoon of oil, olive
- 15 to 20 peeled, deveined shrimp
- 2 tablespoons of pure honey
- 1 teaspoon of minced garlic
- 2 tablespoons of lime juice
- ¼ cup of soy sauce
- 1 teaspoon of pepper, black
- 1 teaspoon of grated ginger

MMMMMMMMMMMMMMMMMMMMMMMMMMMMMMMMM

Methods:

1. Stir pepper, honey, garlic, ginger, lime juice, soy sauce and oil together in a measuring cup. Set aside ½ mixture to brush on shrimp when they are on the grill.

2. Allow shrimp to marinate in the other ½ of mixture for 12-18 minutes.

3. Preheat your grill to med. Thread skewers with pineapple chunks and shrimp alternating.

4. Put skewers on your grill, brushing both sides with extra marinade occasionally. Grill 'til shrimp are pink, which is about three or four minutes on each side.

5. Garnish skewers with chopped mint. Serve.

(26) Aloha Garlic Shrimp

There are many varieties of shrimp served in Hawaii, and you'll find garlic shrimp especially common in food trucks. This recipe is much like the basic recipes used for the type of dish served on the roads in the aloha state.

Yield: 2-4 Servings

Preparation Time: 1/2 hour

List of Ingredients:

- 18 minced cloves of garlic, large
- 2 lbs. of shrimp, jumbo, dried & deveined
- 1 stick of butter, unsalted
- 1 & ½ tablespoons of flour, all-purpose
- 1/3 cup of white wine, dry
- 2 teaspoons of paprika
- 2 tablespoons of oil, olive
- 1 & ½ teaspoons of salt, Hawaiian sea
- ¼ teaspoons of pepper, black

MMMMMMMMMMMMMMMMMMMMMMMMMMMMMMMMM

Methods:

1. Place salt, pepper, paprika and flour in large plastic bowl. Mix until blended well.

2. Add shrimp to mixture and coat well. All of the mixture needs to be used.

3. Set shrimp aside. Allow them to set while you're cooking garlic.

4. Heat 1 tablespoon oil and butter in large sized pan on med-high until butter melts.

5. Add garlic to oil and butter. Cook for a couple minutes until garlic turns light brown.

6. After garlic is light brown, add wine. Cook for a minute or so.

7. Remove garlic sauce from pan. Set it aside.

8. Add other tablespoons of oil to pan. Allow it to get hot. Add shrimp.

9. Cook shrimp for two or three minutes per side. Cooked shrimp will appear pink.

10. Add garlic sauce. Stir. Remove pan from heat and serve.

(27) Pork Tacos & Pineapple Salsa

The crunchy radishes in this Aloha-Mex dish go so well with the sweet pineapple. The slow cooked pork

Yield: these tacos truly mouth-watering.

Yield: 4 Servings

Preparation Time: 4 hours & 15 minutes counting 3-4 hours slow cooker time

List of Ingredients:

- ½ cup of radishes, sliced thinly
- 8 warmed tortillas, corn
- ¼ teaspoons of cumin, ground
- 2 tablespoons of lime juice, fresh
- 2 chopped shallots, medium
- 1 x 7-ounce can of jalapeños, sliced
- 1 pound of pork loin, boneless, raw, cut in four pieces, removed of visible fat
- ½ cup of cubed pineapple, fresh
- 1 & ½ cups of salsa verde

MMMMMMMMMMMMMMMMMMMMMMMMMMMMMMMMMM

Methods:

1. Place the pork, salsa and jalapenos in slow cooker. Cook for three to four hours on high. Pork should shred easily and show no pink.

2. Remove the pork from salsa mixture. Allow to cool for about 20 minutes. Then shred the pork and discard any fat you see.

3. Combine the cumin, lime juice, shallots and pineapple. Combine and set bowl aside.

4. Top tortillas with pork, salsa mixture and radishes. Serve.

(28) Aloha Quesadillas

You may be familiar with Canadian bacon and pineapple on pizzas, but that's not the only recipe in which they work well. This one combines savory and sweet tastes, along with mozzarella cheese, in flavorful, crispy quesadillas.

Yield: 4 Servings

Preparation Time: 25 minutes

List of Ingredients:

- 1 cup of pineapple, chopped
- 8 chopped slices of cooked bacon, Canadian
- 1 lb. of chopped mozzarella cheese
- 8 x 8" tortillas, flour
- 2 tablespoons of oil, vegetable
- 1 pinch red pepper, crushed
- Salt, kosher
- Ground pepper, black

MMMMMMMMMMMMMMMMMMMMMMMMMMMMMMMMMMMMMM

Methods:

1. Arrange four flour tortillas on cutting board. Top them with cheese first, then bacon, followed by pineapple. Season with salt, pepper and red pepper.

2. Heat 2 tablespoons of oil in large sized skillet. Add tops to quesadillas and transfer to skillet. Cook on med-high until they are crisp and golden. This should take a couple minutes on each side. You can add additional oil to your pan if you need it.

3. Transfer quesadillas to work surface. Cut into wedges. Serve promptly with salsa.

(29) Macadamia Mahi Mahi

This Hawaiian recipe offers simply unbelievable taste, by utilizing mainly ingredients native to the islands, but which can be sourced elsewhere. It creates a sweet, hot, succulent entrée that you will watch disappear – quickly.

Yield: 4-6 Servings

Preparation Time: 1 & 1/2 hours

List of Ingredients:

- 1 tablespoon of coconut, shredded,
- 4 oz. of chopped mango
- 2 habanero peppers
- 4 oz. of chopped papaya
- 2 oz. of diced shallots
- 4 oz. of chopped pineapple
- 4 cups of stock, chicken
- 4 oz. of butter, softened
- 6 x 6-oz. of fillets, mahi mahi
- 4 oz. of breadcrumbs, plain
- 2 oz. of macadamia nuts
- Sea salt, ground pepper and white sugar, as desired

MMMMMMMMMMMMMMMMMMMMMMMMMMMMMMM

Methods:

1. Preheat the oven to 375F.

2. Pulse bread crumbs and macadamia nuts in food processor until ground finely. Pour the nut mixture on a plate. Coat both sides of fish fillets.

3. Heat the butter on med. heat in large sized skillet. Fry until both sides are a golden brown in color. Remove to baking pan.

4. Add the shallots to your skillet. Cook until they are translucent and stir in the chicken stock. Add peppers, coconut, mango, papaya and pineapple and mix well. Season using sugar, salt and pepper as desired.

5. Simmer until the sauce thickens, which will take about ½ hour. Strain and remove shallots, peppers and fruit. Reserve sauce in separate pan on low heat.

6. Bake the mahi mahi in the oven for 8 to 10 minutes. Internal temperature should reach 140F. Remove the fillets and coat lightly with the sauce. Serve.

(30) Chicken, Mango & Avocado Hawaiian Salad

Need a wonderful dish for a potluck dinner? Try this Hawaiian salad! It's easy to make, and the only thing you'll need to remember is keeping the salad and dressing separate, so the end result isn't soggy.

Yield: 1 Serving

Preparation Time: 20 minutes

List of Ingredients:

- 3 ounces of cubed chicken breast, skinless, boneless
- ¼ cubed avocado, medium
- 1 tablespoon of vinegar, apple cider
- ¼ cubed, peeled mango, medium
- 2 tablespoons of pineapple juice
- ½ cup of jicama (Mexican yam), cubed
- ¼ cup of pineapple, fresh, cubed
- 1 chopped Serrano chili, medium, seeded
- 1 & ½ teaspoons of oil, olive
- ¼ teaspoons each of cumin, ground; chili powder; sea salt and pepper
- 12 chopped cilantro leaves, fresh

MMMMMMMMMMMMMMMMMMMMMMMMMMMMMMMMM

Methods:

1. Combine oil, vinegar, pineapple juice, salt, pepper, cumin, chili powder and Serrano chili in small sized bowl. Blend by whisking and set bowl aside.

2. Place the chicken, jicama, pineapple, avocado and mango in medium sized bowl and combine well.

3. Drizzle with the dressing and gently toss and blend. Use cilantro to garnish. Serve.

About the Author

A native of Indianapolis, Indiana, Valeria Ray found her passion for cooking while she was studying English Literature at Oakland City University. She decided to try a cooking course with her friends and the experience changed her forever. She enrolled at the Art Institute of Indiana which offered extensive courses in the culinary Arts. Once Ray dipped her toe in the cooking world, she never looked back.

When Valeria graduated, she worked in French restaurants in the Indianapolis area until she became the head chef at one of the 5-star establishments in the area. Valeria's attention to taste and visual detail caught the eye of a local business person who expressed an interest in publishing her recipes. Valeria began her secondary career authoring cookbooks and e-books which she tackled with as much talent and gusto as her first career. Her passion for food leaps off the page of her books which have colourful anecdotes and stunning pictures of dishes she has prepared herself.

Valeria Ray lives in Indianapolis with her husband of 15 years, Tom, her daughter, Isobel and their loveable Golden Retriever, Goldy. Valeria enjoys cooking special dishes in her large, comfortable kitchen where the family gets involved in preparing meals. This successful, dynamic chef is an inspiration to culinary students and novice cooks everywhere.

........●●●●●●●●●●......

Author's Afterthoughts

Thank you for Purchasing my book and taking the time to read it from front to back. I am always grateful when a reader chooses my work and I hope you enjoyed it!

With the vast selection available online, I am touched that you chose to be purchasing my work and take valuable time out of your life to read it. My hope is that you feel you made the right decision.

I very much would like to know what you thought of the book. Please take the time to write an honest and informative review on Amazon.com. Your experience and opinions will be of great benefit to me and those readers looking to make an informed choice.

With much thanks,

Valeria Ray

Printed in Great Britain
by Amazon

49013700R00057